# Silent Battle

*Breaking Cycles.*

*Reclaiming Peace.*

*Becoming Whole.*

Olivia Paisley Troy

This is a work of creative nonfiction based on real experiences. Names, places, and identifying details may have been changed to protect privacy. Any resemblance to actual persons, living or deceased, is coincidental and unintentional.

**Silent Battle**
First Edition, 2025

**ISBN:** 979-8-9936475-0-0

Cover design by Olivia Paisley Troy

For information, visit:
www.OliviaPaisleyTroy.com

Printed in the United States of America

## Table of Contents

*"Some battles are fought in silence,*
*but their victories echo for*
*generations."*
— Olivia Paisley Troy

**Content Advisory:** This novel includes mature themes, including domestic violence and an attempted sexual assault.

## Chapter One: Red Hair and Blue Lights

The man with the long red hair came in like a storm. Not the kind with thunder and rain—but the kind that twists trees out of the ground and leaves everything smelling like metal and panic. He didn't knock when he moved in. He just arrived with a garbage bag of clothes that smelled like mildew, a toolbox, and a grin that didn't reach his eyes.

His name didn't matter—not to me. He was just *him*. The man with the sharp voice, the heavy hands, and the flame-colored hair that blazed beneath the humming kitchen light like something wild that couldn't be tamed.

I was four when my mom's new boyfriend started showing up. Four when I learned to stop asking questions and start listening for danger in footsteps, in door slams, in the pop of a beer can.

He always had a cigarette between his fingers. The smell of smoke and sour beer soaked into our furniture, into the carpets, into my clothes. I could smell him before he even came into the room.

That's when I started hiding in the closet.

It wasn't big, just a narrow strip of space in my bedroom, jammed with my mother's boots, half-broken hangers, and a basket of tangled cords we never used. But it had a door that closed and walls that felt safe—if only because they muffled the sound.

Killer, the dog he brought with him, a Boston terrier, would follow me in.

She'd wedge herself beside me, trembling, her big eyes wide with the kind of fear animals understand better than humans. I'd bury my face in her fur, and she'd press her warm little body against mine like we were both trying to vanish together.
I think she was the only living thing that understood me then. Not in words, but in the way her breath would match mine—quick, shallow, holding, waiting.

Some nights, the fighting started before dinner.
Other times, it waited until after the sun dipped low and the walls turned shadowy. But it always came.
First the yelling—his voice deep and slurred, throwing around curse words I didn't understand but knew were bad because of how they stuck to the air like grease.
Then a crash—maybe a plate, maybe a chair.
Then my mother's voice, pleading, sharp, breaking.

Sometimes I peeked out through the slats in the closet door. I could see the blur of movement, the way he towered over her, the way her arms shielded her head. Once, she fell to the floor and didn't get up right away. That time, I almost screamed.
But Killer licked my hand, and I stayed quiet.

The neighbors always called the police.
Blue and red lights would dance against our front curtains like a twisted party no one wanted to attend. The cops would pound on the door. He'd curse at them too. But eventually, they'd make him leave—stumbling out into the night with his boots untied and his rage spilling behind him.

And then came the quiet. The kind of quiet that hummed like guilt.

It happened so many times I stopped keeping count.
But every time, I'd hope that maybe *this* was the night someone would take me away. Maybe they'd notice the little girl curled in the closet. Maybe they'd look closer, see the dog shaking in my lap, the fear etched into the lines of my tiny face.

They never did.

The cruelest part?
My real father wore a badge.
He was a cop. Not just some stranger—he knew the officers who showed up to our door. Some of them even said his name in hushed tones, like it gave them a reason to tread lighter. Like the fact that *his* daughter lived here made it harder to act.

But he never came.

He never showed up to check if I was okay. Never called to ask what I saw. Never once pulled me out of that house and away from the man with red hair and fists that never stayed still.

That was the beginning of the story.
Not with a birthday. Not with a family photo.
But with a closet, a dog, and the smell of cigarettes curling under the door.

His real name was Michael, but no one ever called him that.
Everyone just called him Red.
Maybe it was his long, blazing hair. Maybe it was the way his anger flared like an open flame. But to me, Red was never a nickname. It was a warning.

No one was safe around him—not even the animals.
Not even the ones who loved the loudest.

## Chapter Two: The Dog That Got Away

Before my parents' divorce, my dad brought home a puppy. She was soft and speckled, with white paws and honey-colored eyes that looked like they understood too much. I named her Riley.

She was my first real friend. The only thing that still felt whole when the rest of the world cracked apart.

She wasn't allowed inside very often. Red made sure of that.

So Riley became my outside dog.

Every morning, she'd be waiting for me when I stepped onto the porch. Her tail would start wagging before the screen door even opened. She followed me around the yard while I played, sat beside me when I picked dandelions from the grass, and watched me with those warm honey-colored eyes.

The yard wasn't much to look at. The grass grew uneven, broken things seemed to collect around the property, and nothing ever felt quite cared for. But somehow Riley made it feel different.

When I was outside with her, I could almost pretend everything was normal.

She'd chase sticks I threw, even when they only landed a few feet away. She'd run after squirrels she never caught and bark proudly as if she'd accomplished something important. Sometimes she'd stretch out in the shade while I sat nearby drawing pictures in the dirt with a stick.

Those moments weren't extraordinary.

That's what made them special.

For a little while, I wasn't thinking about what might happen later. I wasn't listening for shouting or worrying about what kind of mood Red would be in when he got home.

I was just a kid playing with her dog.

Looking back, I think that's why Riley meant so much to me.

She represented the small pieces of childhood that still belonged to me.

Inside the house, there was fear.

Inside the house, there was tension.

Inside the house, there was always the feeling that something bad might happen.

But outside, with Riley running through the grass beside me, life sometimes felt ordinary.

And ordinary was a gift.

When Red's truck pulled into the driveway, Riley always noticed first. Her ears would perk up and she'd stop whatever she was doing. Sometimes she'd stand near me and watch him carefully as he walked toward the house.

She never growled.

She never acted aggressive.

She just watched.

Protective.

Alert.

Loyal.

For a child who didn't feel safe very often, that loyalty meant everything.

I think Riley gave me something I didn't realize I needed at the time.

Consistency.

No matter what happened inside the house, she greeted me the same way every day. She never yelled. She never scared me. She never made me wonder what version of her I was going to get.

She was just Riley.

And in a world that felt unpredictable, that mattered more than I could have understood then.

But Red didn't like her.

He said she was "just a mutt." Said mixed breeds were a waste. He hated how she barked when he raised his voice. He hated how she followed me everywhere.

Most of all, I think he hated that she loved me.

Then one day, Riley was gone.

"She must've run away," my mother told me, eyes red, voice thin. She tried to make it sound like a mystery. A wandering dog story. But I knew better. Riley never even strayed far from our yard.

For days I called for her outside, shaking her little red collar in my hand like it might bring her back.

Every day after school, I searched for her.

I walked the yard calling her name until my voice grew hoarse. I checked beneath porches, around sheds, and along the edge of the woods. Every time I saw movement in the distance, my heart jumped.

Maybe that was her.

Maybe she'd found her way home.

I left food outside and filled a bowl with fresh water every morning. Some part of me believed she'd come back when she was hungry.

Children are remarkably good at hope.

I convinced myself she was lost.

I convinced myself someone had found her.

I convinced myself there was still time.

Weeks passed, but I kept looking.

Whenever I heard a dog bark somewhere in the distance, I stopped and listened. Whenever a car slowed near our house, I looked out the window. Every stray dog I saw made my heart race for a moment.

I was waiting for a miracle.

It never came.

The hardest part wasn't that she was gone.

The hardest part was not knowing.

Not knowing where she was.

Not knowing if she was scared.

Not knowing if she was hungry.

Not knowing if she was waiting for me the same way I was waiting for her.

As the weeks turned into months, I slowly stopped searching every day.

But I never completely stopped hoping.

Part of me kept expecting to look out the window and see her standing there in the yard, tail wagging like she'd only been gone an afternoon.

That hope stayed with me much longer than it should have.

Maybe because Riley wasn't just a dog.

She was one of the few things in my childhood that felt safe.

And when she disappeared, it felt like another piece of safety disappeared with her.

Years later, when I was old enough to read between the lines and silences, I learned the truth. Red didn't just take her away.

He took her out to the woods. Said she'd be better off.

Said she was in the way.

My mother was the one who told me, quietly, one night, when the weight of it finally cracked through her own silence. Her voice shook, her hands twisted in her lap, and I saw it in her eyes before she spoke: the truth.

Riley didn't run away.

She didn't get lost.

Red got rid of her.

And I don't think he just let her go.

Even now, I still hope, somewhere in the soft part of my chest that never grew up, that she made it. That maybe someone found her, took her in, gave her a better life.

Maybe she ended up on a farm somewhere, chasing butterflies through a field and sleeping in the sun.

Maybe she found people who were kind.

People who loved her.

People who would never hurt her.

But the truth whispers otherwise.

And that whisper never really leaves.

Because losing Riley wasn't just losing a dog.

It was losing one of the few things that made childhood feel safe.

She had been proof that loyalty existed.

Proof that love could be simple.

Proof that not everything in my world was broken.

And when she disappeared, something inside me disappeared too.

That was Red.

Destruction wrapped in human skin.

If something brought joy, he found a way to ruin it.

If something made you feel safe, he found a way to take it.

And I was a child learning that the world wasn't safe, not even inside my own home.

Especially not there.

## Chapter Three: When the Sun Went Down

After the first year, I started to know the routine.

The days pretended to be normal—sunlight through the curtains, the hum of cartoons, occasionally having a bowl of cereal when we could afford it, crunching between bites. But behind every moment was a countdown. I didn't look forward to dinner, or bedtime, or weekends.

I only counted down to the dark.

Because darkness meant risk.

By then, I knew what came after the sun went down.

I knew what Red looked like when his voice got low and slurred.

I knew the smell of beer before it even touched his lips.

I knew the sharp sound of a lighter being flicked, the click of his belt, the shuffle of his boots pacing from room to room before it started.

I worried all day about what night would bring.

Would my mother make it through?

Would I?

Fear wasn't something that only showed up at night.

It lived with me all day long.

I'd wake up thinking about bedtime.

I'd sit at school thinking about bedtime.

I'd watch cartoons, eat cereal, or play outside for a little while, and somewhere in the back of my mind the countdown was always there.

How many hours until dark?

How many hours until Red started drinking?

How many hours until the yelling started?

Other kids worried about homework or what they were having for dinner.

I worried about survival.

The hardest part was not knowing.

Some nights were quieter than others. Sometimes Red would disappear for a few hours, and I'd let myself hope maybe he'd stay gone. Sometimes he'd come home in a decent mood and laugh at something on television.

Those nights were almost worse.

Because they tricked you.

They made you believe things might be different.

Then one wrong word.

One wrong look.

One inconvenience.

And the explosion came anyway.

Living that way taught me to constantly scan for danger.

I watched his face.

I listened to the way he shut the refrigerator door.

I paid attention to how hard he set down a beer can.

I could tell the difference between normal footsteps and angry footsteps before I learned multiplication tables.

I didn't know it then, but I was becoming hypervigilant.

At five years old, I was studying human behavior like my life depended on it.

Because sometimes it did.

I started to sleep with my shoes on—just in case I had to run. I made Killer stay close, even though she was growing skittish herself, already aging with the weight of too much fear in too small a body. Her little hips were bad from the many kicks she received from him.

I had little routines that made me feel safer.

Not safe.

Just safer.

I kept my shoes close enough that I could find them in the dark.

Sometimes I slept wearing them.

Sometimes I lined them up beside the bed pointing toward the door.

I don't know why I thought that would help.

Maybe because children create control wherever they can find it.

I memorized the parts of the floor that creaked.

I knew which doors stuck and which ones opened quietly.

I knew where I could hide.

I knew how fast I could get from my room to the closet.

I knew which neighbor's house felt safest if I ever had to run.

Most kids spent their childhood learning games.

I spent mine learning escape routes.

Killer developed routines too.

As evening approached, she'd become restless.

Her ears would twitch at every sound.

Sometimes she'd follow my mother from room to room.

Sometimes she'd sit beside me, watching the door.

Animals know.

They may not understand the details, but they understand fear.

And Killer lived with it just like we did.

And I watched my mother move like a shadow—half there, her nerves constantly stretched, her eyes never really settling.

She knew too.

She always knew.

There was a look she got in the late afternoons.

A tightness around her mouth.

A nervous energy in the way she moved around the kitchen.

She'd glance out the window more often.

Listen for vehicles pulling into the driveway.

Sometimes she'd clean things that were already clean.

Sometimes she'd pace.

Sometimes she'd sit quietly at the table, staring into space as though she was trying to prepare herself for whatever version of Red was coming home that day.

Even as a child, I could feel the tension building before a single word was spoken.

The whole house seemed to know.

When the shouting began, it always escalated fast.

Furniture shook.

Dishes hit the wall.

His voice roared over everything, like a monster that couldn't be reasoned with.

But the part that stays with me more than anything—more than the fists, or the broken glass, or even the closet—is my mother's scream:

"Don't hurt my baby!"

It was the most repeated line of my childhood.

Not "I love you."

Not "Everything's going to be okay."

But "Don't hurt my baby."

She would throw herself over me like a shield.

Tiny, worn down, exhausted—and still somehow braver than anyone I've ever known.

Red would yell louder. Sometimes he'd tell her to shut up, to move. And when she didn't, he'd hit her. Not just slaps. Closed fists. Full force. A grown man swinging at a woman already curled over her child.

What made it all even more heartbreaking was that my mother was disabled. She had only one fully developed arm, the other left half its size from an accident she suffered as a child. And yet, with one strong arm and unshakable love, she shielded me with everything she had.

She took it all to protect me.

I remember the sound more than the sight.

The dull thud of knuckles against flesh.

The gasp that escaped her lips when the air was knocked from her.

The way her body would tense, then tremble, still wrapped around me like armor.

And I'd cry without making noise.

Because even crying felt dangerous.

After the chaos came a strange kind of silence.

A heavy, haunted stillness.

Like the house itself was holding its breath.

If I slept at all, it wasn't really sleep—it was more like collapsing. My little body would shut down from fear, not rest. I'd drift in and out in the closet, curled beside Killer, who trembled the whole time. Even in her sleep, she twitched and whimpered.

We were just two living things trying not to be noticed.

Waking up was the worst part.

Not just because of what had happened, but because I had to face the proof that it really did.

Every morning after a fight felt like waking up on another planet.

The house always looked different.

The mornings carried their own kind of sadness.

Nothing was ever discussed.

No one sat down and talked about what happened.

No apologies were offered.

No explanations were given.

The house simply moved forward as if the night had never existed.

My mother would begin cleaning.

She'd pick up broken glass.

Straighten chairs.

Wipe beer from counters.

Gather pieces of whatever had been destroyed this time.

I used to watch her do it.

The bruises were fresh.

The cuts were fresh.

The pain was fresh.

But the cleanup started anyway.

As if putting the house back together might somehow put us back together too.

Sometimes I'd help.

Not because anyone asked me to.

Because it felt wrong not to.

I'd pick up small pieces of trash.

Move things back where they belonged.

Try to make the room look normal again.

Children shouldn't know how to clean up after violence.

But I did.

The strangest part was how ordinary everything looked afterward.

The sun still came through the windows.

Birds still sang outside.

School buses still drove down the road.

The world kept moving.

It felt impossible to me that life could continue so normally after the things that happened inside our house.

I kept waiting for someone to notice.

For someone to look at my mother and see what I saw.

For someone to ask the right question.

But no one ever did.

Or if they did, they accepted the answers we gave.

And so the cycle continued.

Morning.

Afternoon.

Dread.

Night.

Chaos.

Silence.

Morning again.

Chairs overturned. Picture frames crooked or shattered. Spilled beer dried into the carpet. Sometimes there'd be a bloodstain on the wall. Or on her shirt. Or on the floor by the kitchen table.

I used to stare at the bruises on my mother's face, trying to figure out where one ended and another began. Her eye would be swollen, purple and blue, like something from a Halloween mask. Her lip split. Her arms scraped. Sometimes she limped.

And still, she'd say, "It's okay. It's over."

But it was never really over.

It just paused until the next night.

## Chapter Four: Walking the Line

We didn't have a car.
So every morning, my mother and I walked to school.

Rain, wind, frost—it didn't matter. We bundled up, pulled Killer's leash tight, and trudged down the gravel driveway lined with cigarette butts and broken bottles. Some days, my mother wore sunglasses even when it was cloudy. It wasn't to block the sun. It was to hide the bruises.

She never talked much on those walks.
She kept her eyes on the ground, and her arms tight around herself like she was trying to hold everything in. I walked beside her, quiet too, always glancing behind us, just in case Red decided to follow.

We passed houses with trimmed lawns and mailboxes that weren't dented. Kids got dropped off in cars. Mothers wore clean clothes. Dads kissed foreheads before speeding off to work.
Our world wasn't like that.

My mom didn't work. She couldn't—Red wouldn't allow it, and the bruises didn't heal fast enough for interviews. We lived off of $75 every two weeks. Child support.
Not even enough for groceries.
Some nights, dinner was dry cereal and tap water. Other times, just toast with a little sugar sprinkled on top to make it feel like a treat.

At school, I was the kid who never had lunch money.
The kid whose clothes didn't always fit.
The one who flinched when someone raised their voice or slammed a book too hard. I didn't do well in class.
It wasn't because I didn't care. I did—at least I think I did.

But my brain was always busy scanning for danger. Always listening for footsteps that weren't supposed to be there. Always remembering the bruises I saw that morning, or worrying about what I might come home to.

How do you concentrate on math when your heart still hasn't stopped pounding from the night before?

I fell behind. Every year was a struggle.
Teachers would shake their heads and call me distracted.
Some called me lazy. Others just ignored me.

But none of them knew that I hadn't slept the night before.
That I cried in closets.
That I watched my mom take fists to the face just to keep me from harm.

I wasn't lazy.
I was in survival mode.

And survival doesn't leave much room for multiplication tables or reading logs.

I scraped by. Barely. Passed each grade by the skin of my teeth and the grace of teachers who didn't want to hold back a kid who looked like me—hungry, quiet, tired.

Each year felt like a stolen step. Like I wasn't really moving forward, just dragging my past behind me, heavier every time.

Winter made everything worse.

We still had to walk, same streets, same route—but now the wind cut like knives, and the sidewalks turned slick with ice. My hands would go numb before we even reached the corner, and my nose would run constantly, no tissue, just the back of my sleeve or nothing at all.

I didn't have a proper jacket.
Just a thin zip-up hoodie that hung too short at the wrists and a pair of mismatched gloves we'd found at the thrift store donation bin. My mom tried to layer me in shirts and scarves, but it never worked. The cold always found a way in.

Snow would pile up along the curbs, gray and heavy with car exhaust. My sneakers that were way too small soaked through within minutes. I remember the squish of wet socks, the sting of frozen toes, and the burning feeling in my ears when the wind slapped against them.

I was sick a lot.
Colds that never quite went away.
Coughing fits that rattled my ribs.
A throat so sore some mornings I could barely speak, but we still walked. Always walked.

I remember one morning in particular—the sky was that dull, colorless gray that looks like it's holding back a storm. I was shivering so hard my teeth wouldn't stop chattering, and just as we turned down the long stretch of road toward the school, I sneezed so violently that it felt like my whole face cracked. The cold made everything hurt. My skin, my lungs, my bones. Even breathing burned.

But I didn't complain. I never did.
What was the point?

My mom would glance down at me with that look she wore every day—a mixture of guilt, fear, and love knotted so tightly together it looked like pain.

I think she knew I was suffering.
I think she was too. But when survival is your only goal, comfort becomes a luxury you forget how to want.

When I finally got to school, my face would be red and raw, sleeves stiff with frozen snot. I'd huddle near the heater vents while the other kids pulled off warm coats and laughed like the air didn't hurt them.

No one ever asked why I didn't have a jacket.
No one asked why I missed so many days.
No one asked why I always looked tired and pale.

Maybe they thought I was just one of those kids who didn't try.

But the truth was, I tried so hard just to get there.
And some days, that was the bravest thing I did.

Coming home didn't bring the kind of relief it should have.
There was no warmth waiting.
No fire in the fireplace, no hot cocoa, no dry socks.
Just more cold.

Our tiny house was old—older than it looked, older than the memories inside it. The walls were thin enough to hear the wind whistle straight through the gaps. The windows had frost on the inside. The floor stayed cold no matter how many towels we layered across it. We didn't have a real heater, just space heaters that barely buzzed, and they couldn't keep up with the Tennessee winters that came in sharp and stayed too long.

At some point, someone gave my mom a kerosene heater.
It was dented and rusted, but it worked—kind of.

She set it in my bedroom at night, careful to keep it away from the blankets. The smell was awful—thick and oily, the kind that sat in the back of your throat—but it was the closest thing to warmth we had. I used to fall asleep staring at the blue glow of its flame, listening to it tick and click and hum as it pushed out tiny bursts of heat.

But even with it on, the house was never warm. Not really.

As a kid, winter usually meant sledding and snowmen and frozen fingers warmed by mugs of something sweet. For other kids, it was joy. For me, it was dread.

Because when you don't have a way to get warm, the snow isn't magical.
It's just cruel.

I didn't play outside in it. I walked through it. I stood in it waiting for the school doors to open. I scraped it off my shoes with numb fingers and watched it melt into my sleeves because there wasn't anywhere dry to put my coat. I didn't build snow forts or catch flakes on my tongue—I curled into corners and tried not to shake so hard that it made people stare.

Tennessee winters hit different when you knew the cold didn't stop outside.
It followed you in.
It wrapped around your bones at night.
It made a home inside your skin.

I learned to hold my breath when the cold felt unbearable.
Just pause.
Wait.
Survive.

That's what I did best.

## Chapter Five: Skates and Sanctuary

Not everything from that time was pain.
There were cracks in the darkness where the light got in.
And for me, one of those cracks lived just a few houses down—in the form of a brick building with chipped paint, a humming soda machine, and laughter that spilled out into the street.
The community center.

Even though we lived in a poor neighborhood, the one thing we had was *each other.* The neighbors looked out for one another. You didn't have much, but you shared what you could. We all knew who was struggling. And when the screams from my house got too loud, nobody asked questions. But they noticed. They *cared*—especially Ms. Bland.

The community center was my escape.
Any chance I got, I'd run down there—whether it was to avoid a fight, hide from the cold, or just pretend for a few hours that I was like every other kid. In the summer, they had free lunches—ham sandwiches, milk, and fruit cocktail in plastic cups. I had never had fruit until the free lunches. I remember sitting on the floor in front of the box fan, cooling off after playing dodgeball, the taste of the tiny diced fruit still in my mouth.
It felt like safety.
It felt like *belonging.*

And on the weekends? Roller skating.

The center had an old wooden basketball court, and they'd turn it into a skating rink. The music would echo off the walls—pop songs and funky beats. We'd skate in circles for hours, chasing each other, laughing, falling and laughing again.

That's where I learned to skate.
Not just stand up on wheels, but *really* skate—gracefully, confidently, fast and free. I was good at it. Still am.
Skating was the first time I felt like I could fly.
Like I was in control of something.
Like I had power in my legs and rhythm in my bones and joy in my chest.
Even if just for a little while.

And then there was Ms. Bland.

She was the heart of that place.
Kind, warm, always dressed in earth tones and always smelling like cocoa butter and peppermint. She *knew*. She never said much about it, but she *knew* what was going on at home.

She'd sneak me snacks—little bags of cookies, peanut butter crackers, juice boxes tucked in my backpack when no one was looking. She'd check in with me when I came in, run her hand across my back, look me in the eyes, and ask how I was really doing.

And sometimes—when she knew my mom couldn't feed me, or the lights were out again—she'd take me out.

Not in a flashy way. Just little acts of kindness that meant the world to a kid who never had much. She took me to the diner once and let me order whatever I wanted. I picked pancakes even though it was dinnertime, breakfast was rarely served in my home so it was a must-try, just because I could.
She took me to the mall for the first time in my life.

I remember staring at the escalator, scared to get on, and she just smiled and held my hand until I took that first step. She took me to the wave pool once too—I screamed and laughed and forgot about everything else for a whole afternoon.

She gave me more than food.
She gave me *moments*.
Moments where I felt seen. Safe. Loved.

Ms. Bland didn't save me from everything.
But she reminded me that goodness existed.
That some people chose kindness, even when the world didn't give them much to work with.

I don't know where I'd be without that community center.
Without her.

There was one more person who made those days bearable—my best friend, Daniel.

He lived right across the street, in a house not as weathered as ours. Daniel was only a year older than me, but he always felt braver—like he knew how to carry both of our fears without breaking.

He was my everything.

We played every chance we got.
Building forts from sticks and scrap wood, climbing trees like we were chasing the sky, running through the neighborhood until our legs gave out. His backyard had an old swing set with squeaky chains, and we'd take turns pushing each other so high the sky tilted.
We laughed loud.
We forgot things.

Daniel knew what was happening in my house—he didn't need the full story. He could hear it. Sometimes he'd see me sitting on the curb afterward, face blotchy, shoulders small.
He never asked.
He just sat beside me.
And when we were alone, he'd lean close and say,

"One day I'm gonna beat up that red-headed guy. I'll make sure he never touches you again."

We were just kids—skinny, wide-eyed, and barely old enough to know how to fight.
But he meant it.
In the way only children can mean something, with every part of their heart.

I think Daniel understood that I needed someone to believe in me.
To see me as more than the girl from the broken house.
With him, I wasn't a victim.
I was a teammate. A co-adventurer. A tree climber. A skater. A friend.

We'd run around the community center until dusk. Hide behind the bushes, chase each other with sticks, laugh until our stomachs ached.
We told stories like we'd live in them forever.

Even when my world felt like it was falling apart, Daniel helped stitch it back together, piece by piece, with forts and swings and promises only best friends can make.

There weren't a lot of good memories from that time.
But the ones I *do* have—Daniel is in most of them.

Sometimes, when the sun started to dip behind the rooftops and the cicadas began to sing, I'd wish time would just stop right there—Daniel still laughing beside me, my skates slung over my shoulder, Ms. Bland calling out the community center doors to remind us it was closing time.

Those moments were golden.
Not because everything was perfect, but because I got to *forget.*
I got to be a kid.
Just a kid.

But eventually, the streetlights would flicker on.
The other kids would go home to warm houses and dinner on the stove.
Daniel would wave goodbye from his porch and disappear inside.

And I'd start the slow walk back.
Each step heavier than the last.

I remember those walks clearly—the quiet dread creeping back in, the shift in my shoulders as I crossed that invisible line from freedom to fear. The air felt colder on my street. The shadows longer. The house darker than it should've been.

I'd open the front door carefully, holding my breath.
Sometimes it was quiet.
Sometimes the storm had already started.

The smell would hit me first—alcohol, smoke, and something sharp I never could name.
My mother might be on the couch, curled up in silence.
Red might be in the kitchen, already muttering, already swaying.

And I would take off my shoes slowly, like noise might set the world off again.
Like if I moved just right, I could stay invisible.

Because no matter how high I'd soared that day with Daniel on the swings, or how fast I skated around the gym floor, or how full Ms. Bland made my heart with her kindness—

I still had to go home.

## Chapter Six: The Edge of Knowing

As the years passed, the bruises grew darker, the silence heavier, and my understanding sharper.

The older I got, the clearer things became.
At first, I thought the violence was random. A bad day, too many drinks, a slammed door that triggered something ugly.
But by the time I was eight, I knew better.
This wasn't chaos.
This was *who he was.*

There were stretches when Red would vanish—disappear for a week, sometimes longer. The air would lighten. My mom would sleep a little deeper. I'd laugh more, even let myself feel okay for a moment. But he always came back.

Always.

With his battered old toolbox, his cartons of cigarettes, and a bottle in each hand like they were part of his bones. No warning. No knock. Just the door swinging open, and with it, the fear flooding in all over again.

As the abuse got worse, it also got more complicated.
More unpredictable.
It wasn't just fists anymore. It was slammed doors, shattered dishes, broken things that used to matter—us included.

One night, I watched it happen in slow motion.

My mom stood in the doorway, blocking him from coming toward me. He was drunk, stumbling, shouting, his face twisted and red. And then—without hesitation—he slammed the glass door right onto her.
The shattering sound of glass was deafening.

She fell back, blood immediately blooming across her arms, her hands, her chest. Deep, angry gashes that looked too big for one body to hold. I froze—every part of me turned to ice.

And that's when I saw them.
The frying pans.

My mom had them hanging on the wall—the way so many women in Tennessee did, cast iron and blackened with years of use. Heavy. Real. Weapons, if they had to be.

And all I could think was:

*Grab one. Hit him. Hit him in the head. Stop this. Make it stop.*

I could see it play out in my head—me, leaping forward, swinging with everything I had, like in a movie where the little girl finally gets her revenge.
But even in my eight-year-old mind, I knew the truth:
I couldn't do it.
Not hard enough to make a difference.
Not without him turning on me.

And if he turned on me that night, I didn't think I'd survive it.

Later, when the blood had been cleaned and the shouting dulled into silence, I stood in the kitchen and looked at those pans again.
I hated them.
Not because they didn't help.
But because they reminded me of how powerless I still was.

Then came the night he grabbed me.

It wasn't even during a full-blown fight—just one of those sudden bursts of rage that hit without warning. He gripped my arm like it wasn't even attached to me and flung me across the room so hard that the wall seemed to catch me like a wave crashing into shore.

Pain bloomed immediately. My shoulder screamed. My mom screamed louder.

We ran.

She didn't pack a bag. We just ran. Straight to a friend's house. Her name slips from my memory, but her face—her *face*—I'll never forget.

She looked at me with wide, horrified eyes and ushered us inside without asking questions. I sat curled on her couch, clutching my arm and trying not to cry. My mother looked broken, guilt dripping from her like sweat.

That night, I went to the ER. I don't remember much about the visit. I don't remember anyone asking me what happened. Maybe they did. Maybe I was too scared to answer.
But I know my mom lied.
She always did.

No X-rays. No real exam.
Just a doctor's glance, a shrug, and a discharge slip.

But I remember the look on my mom's friend's face.
Disgust. Worry.
The kind of expression that sticks with you longer than any bruise.

It said what no one else ever did:

*This is not okay.*
*You shouldn't have to live like this.*
*You are a child, and this should not be your life.*

## Chapter Seven: The Bone Beneath It All

The night Red slammed me into the wall stayed with me long after the bruises faded.
What we didn't realize—what none of us saw then—was that something inside me had broken in more ways than one.

At first, it just felt like soreness. A pulled muscle. I favored my shoulder, flinched when someone brushed against it, but I said nothing. We were used to not talking about pain.
But the pain never left. It didn't dull. It stayed sharp, tucked beneath the skin like a secret.

That summer, my mom and I left Tennessee to stay with my aunt and uncle in Texas.

They were a godsend.
They bought the plane tickets. They made sure we had meals, clean sheets, and laughter around the table. My uncle told corny jokes that actually made me laugh. My aunt bought me coloring books and sat with me while I filled in the pages, praising every scribbled masterpiece like it belonged in a museum.

For the first time in forever, I felt safe.

It was like breathing fresh air after being stuck in a smoke-filled room.
I slept better, even if my shoulder still ached.
I ate full meals. I laughed. I let myself relax, just a little.

But one night, I rolled too close to the edge of the bed and fell.

It wasn't far—just a small drop to the floor—but I landed hard on the same shoulder. And the pain that ripped through me was like lightning.

I woke up screaming.
Tears poured down my face before I even understood what had happened.
My aunt and uncle rushed in, and my mom followed, tired and disoriented. But no one took me to the hospital. No one asked for X-rays. My mother cradled me, shushed me, and tucked me back in gently like that would fix what was inside.

I didn't understand why.
I didn't know that my mom was afraid.
Not just afraid of the injury—but afraid of what a doctor might *see*. What they might report. What it might mean.

It wasn't until years later that I put the pieces together.
She didn't take me because she thought if anyone found out how it had happened… she might lose me.
And in her broken, frightened way, she thought she was protecting me.

But that shoulder—my shoulder—was never the same.

At the end of summer, we packed up our bags, and all the warmth of Texas was left behind.

We landed back in Tennessee and walked into the airport with heavy hearts.
And there he was.
Red.

Waiting at the gate like nothing had happened.
Like we hadn't escaped. Like he hadn't shattered everything.

The moment I saw him, a chill ran through me—not just fear, but *dread.*
I felt sick.
The pain in my shoulder flared up again, sharp and cruel, like it knew exactly what we were walking back into.

He smiled like we were some happy little family returning from vacation.
I wanted to disappear.

The next week, my mom took me to the doctor for the mandatory back-to-school checkup. I didn't expect anything. It was routine—something every kid had to do.

But when the doctor asked me to lift my arms, I winced.
He paused. Asked again.
Then gently touched my shoulder. I flinched so hard I almost slid off the table.

That's when they found it.
A broken collarbone. Torn ligaments. Some of the damage had been there for months.

I had to wear a shoulder brace—one of those rigid ones that wraps across your back and pulls your posture into place whether you want it to or not.
It itched. It restricted everything.
And yet, in a strange way, it was the only *proof* I had that what happened to me was real.

There was something about that brace that stuck with me.
Maybe because for once, my pain wasn't invisible.
Maybe because for once, someone believed me—without me even having to explain.

I wore that brace for a long time.

Even with the broken shoulder, even with the pain that stitched itself into my bones, I stayed strong. I don't know how.
Maybe it was the parts of me that refused to break.
Maybe it was the borrowed love from people like Ms. Bland or Daniel.
Or maybe it was something else—something in me that knew, even then, this couldn't be forever.

Our new escape wasn't quiet.
It wasn't planned.
It was running—in the dark, in the cold, in pajamas that barely kept out the night air.
My mom and I would wait until Red passed out or left for a beer run, and then we'd go. No shoes sometimes. No bags. Just fear in our throats and a direction in our feet: *away*.

We'd hide at a friend's house. Sleep on a couch. Pretend we were just visiting.
And always, eventually, we'd return.
Because where else could we go?

One afternoon, I was next door playing with the kids who lived there—three of them, with bikes in the yard and cartoons playing too loud. It felt normal. Safe. I could hear laughter in the background, and for a second I forgot about Red completely.

Then his voice shattered everything.

He stormed into their front yard, red-faced and wild, screaming my name like I belonged to him. Screaming for me to come home, to stop hiding, to face him.

I froze. The kids froze. The older brother ran to the front door and slammed it shut.

We locked everything—the door, the windows, even the back gate. I remember crouching in their hallway, holding my breath as his shadow passed by the windows. He was pounding on the door, yelling curses, threatening everyone.

And like always, the neighbors called the police.

The neighbors always called.

Because we couldn't.
We didn't *have* a phone.

There was one once—an old rotary with a spiral cord that sat on the kitchen wall when Red first moved in. I used to spin the dial for fun, listening to the soft click as the numbers returned to place. But after the first few violent nights, the phone disappeared. Just gone.
No explanation.
No warning.
No help.

The positive part of me wanted to think that it was gone because she couldn't pay the bill, but in reality, that's not what happened.

It vanished along with every ounce of safety.

Red didn't want us to have a way out.
He didn't want help to be an option.
So the only hope we had were the neighbors—always listening, always watching, always stepping in when it got too loud to ignore.

It's strange how something like that can feel both comforting and humiliating.
I was grateful someone heard us. Grateful someone cared

enough to call.
But also… ashamed.
Ashamed of how many times it must have happened.
Ashamed that our emergencies became their routine.

Even now, I wonder how many phone calls they made across those years.
How many times officers pulled into our driveway, lights flashing across the broken blinds.

But still—my mother never pressed charges.
Never had him arrested.
Never cut him off for good.

I used to ask myself why.
Was it fear? Guilt? Denial?

Or maybe it was something colder—maybe it was survival.
Maybe she didn't want to work. Maybe she couldn't.
Maybe Red's tiny paycheck and broken promises were still more than what she thought she could do on her own.

That thought haunted me for years:

*Did she let him stay so we could just barely get by?*
*Was the violence the price of rent?*

There are no easy answers.
Only memories.
Some stitched together by silence.
Some shattered like that glass door.

But I survived.
Broken shoulder. Broken home. Broken rules.

I survived them all.

## Chapter Eight: Sleep Is the Enemy

Emotionally, I held everything in.

Not because I wanted to be brave, but because there was no room for emotion.
Crying didn't help. Talking didn't help.
Tears just made him angrier, and words were dangerous.
So I learned to shut it all down.
I became still.
Silent.

Mentally, I stayed alive by staying *awake*.

If I didn't sleep, I couldn't be caught off guard.
If I kept my eyes open, I could listen—track his footsteps, calculate the distance between his rage and my door, be ready to run.
If I stayed awake, I was *safe*.

That was my logic at eight years old.

Some kids stayed up late watching cartoons or reading under the covers.
I stayed up to survive.

My body learned how to function on two hours of sleep. My eyes memorized every shadow in my room. My mind rehearsed escape routes like prayers—closet, window, back door, neighbor's yard.

Always ready.
Always tense.

Because one night, something worse happened.
Worse than the shouting.
Worse than the fists.

It was late. The house was dark and heavy, that kind of silence that makes your skin crawl.
I was half-asleep, too tired to keep my eyes open, when I felt the shift in the air. A creak on the floorboards. Breath that wasn't mine.

And then—Red.
In my doorway.
In my room.

He crossed the space between us like a shadow—slow, drunk, certain.
He sat on the edge of my bed and reached toward me with hands that had no right.

My heart exploded in my chest.
I froze.

But then something in me snapped into motion—pure survival. I kicked. I screamed. I rolled out of bed and ran, barefoot and shaking, straight into my mother's room. I don't remember what I said. I just remember how cold the floor felt and how loud my heartbeat was in my ears.

She screamed at him.
Slammed the door.
Locked us in.

That night, I didn't sleep at all.
I stared at the ceiling, body curled into itself, trying to erase the feeling of his presence from my skin. But it never really left.

After that, I stopped sleeping for real.

Because now sleep wasn't just unsafe—it was *dangerous.*
It was when your guard was down. When your door didn't matter.
When the worst things could happen in the quiet.

And while I sat there in the dark, my house began to slowly disappear.

Piece by piece.
The broken things never got replaced. The furniture dwindled.
First it was a broken chair, then a lamp knocked over in a fight.
The TV got cracked. The mirror shattered. Picture frames tossed like frisbees during one of his rages.

It was like living inside a slow-motion disappearing act.
A vanishing home.
Everything that made it feel like a real place… gone.

All that was left was the fear.

And it kept getting worse.

Red's threats turned darker, sharper, more specific.
He stopped just hitting and screaming. He started *promising* things.

"One day I'm gonna kill that little girl."
"You think you can hide her forever?"
"I'll put her in the ground."

He'd say it casually, like it was just another insult.
But every time, my stomach dropped.
And every time, my mother would explode.

She used to protect me with her body.
Now she tried to protect me with her voice—yelling back, clawing at him, throwing herself into fights she couldn't win.

It got to her.

She started drinking. First just a little. Then more.
At first, I thought it was just exhaustion, or sadness. But it turned into something else—something numbing and hollow.
She wasn't drinking to celebrate.
She was drinking to forget.
To survive.

My protector became her own prisoner.

I remember the moment I realized she wasn't going to save us anymore.
It wasn't loud.
It wasn't dramatic.
It was the stillness in her eyes, the way she stared past me, drink in hand, while Red yelled in the background.
She was gone, even though she was right there.

And me?
I kept watching.
Waiting.
Wondering.

*Would it ever stop?*
*Would we ever escape for good?*

Sometimes I think about those early years—those first nine. And I ask myself the same question over and over:

*How did I survive that?*

Not just the bruises.
Not just the hunger or the cold.
Not even just the pain.

But the fear.
The constant, gnawing fear.

The kind that crawls into your bones and builds a home there.
The kind that makes sleep your enemy.
That turns bedtime into battle.

And I still don't know the answer.

But I did survive.
Broken shoulder. Broken home. Broken rules.
Even *that.*

I survived them all.

Looking back, it's hard to explain what it feels like to live without a future.

To exist in a world so unstable, so filled with chaos, that dreaming becomes a threat—something too tender to touch, too dangerous to hope for.
You learn not to imagine.
Not to plan.
Not to reach.

But even in that emptiness, something in me kept going.
Maybe it was instinct.
Maybe it was the tiniest spark of something I couldn't name.
Not hope, exactly—just… resistance.

A refusal to give up.
A quiet, stubborn ember buried deep beneath the rubble.

And somehow, that ember carried me to the summer of 1992.

## Chapter Nine: A Different Kind of Quiet

It was the summer of 1992, and I was nine years old when my mom and I left Tennessee again—headed for Texas.

But this time, we didn't fly.

My uncles came to get us themselves, driving all the way from Texas in a big RV that rumbled down our cracked street like a rescue mission on wheels. I remember the way it hissed when they parked in front of our house, the way the door creaked open, and how their faces were full of warmth, already pulling us into safety before we'd even stepped inside.

That's the day they met Red.

They'd heard stories, pieced together through my mother's nervous voice over the payphone and letters, but now they were face to face with him.
Red stood on the porch like he owned the place—arms crossed, eyes cold, cigarette balanced between two fingers.
I don't remember what was said. I just remember the tension in the air—sharp and heavy. My uncles didn't flinch, but I could see it in their eyes: they saw everything they needed to see.

And he saw it too.
He saw that they weren't afraid of him.
That they weren't like everyone else who turned away.

I don't know if Red said goodbye.
I don't remember him at all once we climbed into the RV.
All I remember is the door shutting, the engine rumbling,

and that feeling in my chest—the feeling that maybe, just maybe, we were pulling away from something that wouldn't follow us this time.

Not long into the trip, the RV's air conditioner broke.
It sputtered and died somewhere in the middle of nowhere, leaving us to crawl through the humid Southern heat like we were driving through an oven on wheels.
The air was thick and sticky. Sweat rolled down my back.
My legs stuck to the vinyl seats, and everything smelled like gas, old plastic, and summer dust.

But I didn't care.
I didn't care at all.

The heat was awful—but *freedom* was better.
Every mile between me and that house in Tennessee was a gift.
Every drop of sweat felt like proof:

*You're getting out. You're going somewhere safe.*

I sat near the window with the hot breeze hitting my face and felt something close to peace.
No yelling.
No crashing.
No footsteps to track.
Just road, sky, and distance.

It was the kind of ride you don't forget.
Because even though I was drenched in heat, for the first time in my life—I wasn't drowning in fear.

That was the best summer of my childhood.
No question.
No comparison.

For the first time, I wasn't surviving—I was *living.*

Texas felt like another planet. A world where people laughed without flinching, where the only yelling came from someone cheering you on in a pool game or calling you to dinner.
It felt like real life was happening—and somehow, I had been invited.

We ate *so good.*
My aunt could cook like nobody else. Big Southern meals—fried chicken, green beans with bacon, cornbread that melted on your tongue. My uncle grilled ribs so tender they fell off the bone. Every bite felt like love.
And after dinner? Mint chocolate chip ice cream. Always mint.
It became our little tradition—sticky bowls, laughter, green tongues, full hearts.

I swam in my uncle's pool, the water sparkling like freedom under the Texas sun.
We blasted music from the back porch speakers—oldies, country, pop, anything with a beat—and danced around the yard barefoot, twirling like the world wasn't broken.

For once, it wasn't.

No one was breaking furniture.
No one was screaming threats.
No one was bleeding or hiding or lying or bracing for what came next.

We just *were.*
Happy.
Fed.
Safe.

Even my mom changed in those weeks.
She smiled more. Laughed louder. Her eyes looked younger.
She wasn't drinking as much. She wasn't broken.
She was *still in there*, and I could see her.

And me?
I began to learn what joy felt like.
Not just relief from fear—but real, full-bodied joy.
Floating in the pool, music in my ears, ice cream on my tongue, sun on my skin.

There were no clocks. No bruises. No nightmares.

But underneath it all, there was something else too—quiet, steady, heavy:

The knowing.

The knowing that summer wouldn't last forever.
That eventually, school would start.
That eventually, we'd have to go back.

Back to Tennessee.
Back to that house.
Back to *him*.

Every beautiful day was followed by a tiny knot in my stomach.
Every night under the stars came with the quiet dread of the end of summer.

It was the happiest I had ever been—
and still, Red waited like a shadow at the edge of everything.

The night before we were supposed to fly back to Tennessee, everything caught up with me.

The dread I'd been holding in all summer finally spilled out the moment I stepped into the shower. I tried to be quiet—I always did—but the tears came hard and fast, and I couldn't stop them. My whole body shook with sobs I didn't even understand. It felt like saying goodbye to the only life I ever wanted.

The water ran hot, but it didn't comfort me.
I cried so hard I scared my aunt.
She knocked on the bathroom door gently, her voice soft and worried.
When I didn't answer, she opened it just enough to call my name again.
And I remember seeing her face through the steam—eyes wide, hand pressed to her chest like my pain had hit her there.

I think in that moment they all realized I couldn't go back.
Not like before.
Not without a way out.

That's when the plan was made.

I truly believe they had already been talking behind the scenes—my aunt, my uncle, maybe even my mom. But that night, when they saw how broken I was, how terrified, they brought me into it.
They told me, gently and clearly:

"We're going back for now.
But this is the last chance.
If Red lays a hand on anyone—if he *even tries*—we'll put you both on a plane and bring you right back here.
Forever."

It wasn't the perfect solution.
But it was *something.*
A line drawn in the sand.
A promise I could hold onto in the darkest moments.

I didn't want to leave.
My heart ached at the thought of saying goodbye to the pool, the mint ice cream, the music, the laughter.
But knowing I had a way back—a plan, a path, a door out—made the leaving just barely bearable.

That night, I didn't sleep much.
None of us did.

But for the first time in my life, I wasn't walking into the fire blind.
I had a match.
A map.
And people who wouldn't let me burn alone.

## Chapter Ten: The Emergency in Every Day

Stepping back into that house felt like a nightmare.

Everything good I had felt in Texas drained from my body the second the front door opened. It was like the walls breathed differently—heavier, meaner. The air smelled like rot, sweat, and something sour that lived deep in the floors.

The grass in the yard had grown so tall it looked like a forest.
Thick and wild. Untouched.
Like no one had cared for anything all summer long.
Like no one had noticed we were gone—or worse, like someone had waited.

Inside, it was worse.

The house was overrun.
Rats skittered along the baseboards at night. Roaches crawled in the open. Fleas bit at our ankles in every room. I remember scratching until my skin was raw, crying in silence so I wouldn't wake him up.

I had just spent the best summer of my life—filled with sunshine, pool water, music, laughter—and now I was back in this.

Back in filth.
Back in fear.
Back in the belly of the thing I thought I'd escaped.

I wanted to be in Texas so badly it hurt.
And the only way I knew how to reach it—how to feel *safe*—was the pay phone at the community center.

They had taught me how to call collect.
I remembered the steps like a prayer:
Pick up. Dial zero. Say my name fast when prompted.
"Olivia. It's me. I'm okay. Call me back."

And I did it repetitively the entire first day we were back.

I knew I wasn't supposed to.
Collect calls were expensive. They said to use it only for emergencies.
But what they didn't understand—what I couldn't explain—was that every single day was an emergency for me.

Every day I spent in that house was a code red.
Every hour I made it through was a siren in my chest.

Sometimes they answered. Sometimes they couldn't.
But just hearing their voices—my aunt's soft "Hi, baby" or my uncle's steady "How's my girl?"—made me feel like the world hadn't disappeared completely.

It was my safety net.
A lifeline stretched all the way across the miles.

Just hearing their voices reminded me:
There's a place where I am loved.
There's a place where I can breathe.
There's a place—far away, but real—where I am *safe*.

When we got home from Texas, I never unpacked.

I didn't see the point.
Unlike my mother, I *knew* it would happen again.

I was only nine years old, but five years in that house had taught me more than most adults ever have to learn. People don't change just because you hope they will. Monsters don't become gentle just because they're given one more chance.

Red wasn't going to change.
And deep down, I think we all knew it.

What made this time any different?

It only took *two days.*

Two days for the horror to return.
The screaming, the fists, the shattered glass.
The little bit of peace that had lingered from Texas—gone.

Our house, already broken, now felt like a hollow shell of what it once tried to be.
Bare walls. Fleas biting at our skin. Roaches crawling without fear.
Rats in the corners.
And rage in the air.

I remember the sound of something crashing—maybe a lamp, maybe a bottle. I remember my mother's voice screaming in panic, in fury, in *defeat.*

And that was it.

I didn't wait for permission.
I didn't wait to be saved.

I grabbed my still-packed Texas bag and *ran.*

In the middle of the night, barefoot and shaking, I bolted across the footbridge that connected to the main road. That footbridge went across the gulley that I played in and caught crawdads. This time on the footbridge I ran like it was a highway out of hell. I didn't stop. I didn't look back. I just ran, that bag thumping against my side with every stride—my last connection to the place I needed to be.

I didn't know where I was going.
But I knew exactly what I was running from.

My mom caught up with me eventually—frantic, breathless.
But something had changed in her face.
She saw it.
She *felt* it.
Maybe she needed to see me running like that to understand it was finally time.

That night, she found a family willing to take me in. Strangers who opened their door at midnight and wrapped me in safety I didn't even know how to accept.

And within 48 hours—
I was on a plane.
Back to Texas.

This time, my mom kept the promise.

There was no "maybe if," no second chance for Red, no excuses.

She stayed behind for a while.
But she sent *me* to safety.
She let me go.

I watched Tennessee disappear beneath the clouds from my seat on the plane, my bag in my lap, and my heart pounding in a way I couldn't explain.
I didn't cry.
I didn't smile.
I just stared out the window and breathed.

Because for the first time in my life…
I was going home.

## Chapter Eleven: The Beginning of After

Texas felt different this time.

Not like a vacation.
Not like an escape.
But like something permanent. Something real. Something I could start to trust.

There was no plan for how long I'd stay.
There wasn't a script for how to start over.
But I unpacked my bag this time—and that said everything.

My aunt and uncle welcomed me back like I had never left.
They didn't ask for explanations.
They didn't need details.
They just saw me for what I was: a child who needed to heal.

And so, they gave me the one thing I had never had before: *stability*.

Meals at the table.
Music in the background.
Laughter that didn't sting.

I slept in a real bed, in a clean room, without fear.
The first few nights were rough—I still stayed up too late, listening for footsteps, checking the shadows.
But slowly, I stopped flinching at every creak.
I started letting my body rest.

That was new.
Letting myself *rest*.

I didn't wake up to yelling.
I woke up to food.
I woke up to sunlight.

There was a rhythm to life now—slow, safe, predictable. We went grocery shopping and ran errands together. I swam in the pool again, but this time without the weight of dread pressing behind every stroke.

Sometimes my mom would write me a letter.
I worried about her.
I didn't know how she was holding up, what she was still dealing with, or when she would come.
But I knew this time was different.

Because I had *left*.
And she had let me go.

School started eventually.
It was hard at first—new kids, new routines, new everything.
I was quiet, older than my age in some ways and far behind in others.
But for the first time, I had a shot.
A real shot at learning, healing, becoming something more than what had been done to me.

I still didn't know what I wanted to be when I grew up.
But I finally believed I *might* grow up.

There were still scars.
Still shadows.
But the fear wasn't in every corner anymore.
It faded, slowly, like bruises in the sun.

Texas became my reset button.
Not perfect.
But possible.

It was the beginning of *after*.
After Red.
After fear.
After silence.

It was where I began to learn who I really was—
not just the girl who survived.
But the girl who could finally begin to *live*.

The transition to normalcy wasn't easy.

Texas was safe—but safety didn't erase the fear right away.
It didn't flip a switch and make me a whole child again.

Just days after landing, I was enrolled in school.
No time to process. No time to settle in.
Just a new classroom, new kids, new rules—and me, dropped into the middle of it like I was supposed to know how to be normal.

I started fifth grade that week.
It was rough.

Better than what I came from, sure.
But still hard in all the ways that no one could see.

The teachers weren't cruel—but they weren't always kind, either.
They made jokes about my accent—called it "hillbilly," teased the way I said certain words.
I laughed along sometimes, because what else could I do?
At least they weren't hitting me.

At least I didn't have to go home and listen for footsteps at night.

So, I took the teasing.
I swallowed it down like old medicine.
Because ridicule was easier than fists.
And embarrassment was easier than bruises.

But still… it hurt.

Every morning was a battle.

Not with the world—but with myself.

I would wake up and hide in the closet.
Same one I kept my shoes in.
Same one where my Texas bag had finally been unpacked.
I'd sit in the corner, knees to chest, afraid to move.

It wasn't school I feared.
It was *leaving* my aunt and uncle.
Leaving safety.
Leaving the only people who had ever shown me what unconditional love looked like.

I was terrified the world outside their door would break me again.
That it would swallow me up, just like Tennessee did.

Because out there, harm didn't always come in fists.
Sometimes it came in sharp words and teasing.
Sometimes in silence.
Sometimes in the subtle way people made you feel like you didn't belong—even after you fought like hell to be somewhere better.

My uncle would find me sometimes, curled up in the closet, dressed but unmoving.
He never rushed me.
He'd kneel down, and whisper, "You have to go to school."
And eventually, I'd rise.
Put on my backpack.
Walk out the door.

But I carried the fear with me.
Tucked deep in my chest, quiet and familiar.

Because even in a better place, it takes a long time to unlearn what survival taught you.

I never told anyone why I didn't want to go to school.

Not the teachers.
Not the counselor.
Not even the kind ones who seemed like they might understand.

No one ever knew the real reason I hid in the closet each morning.
Why I flinched at loud voices.
Why I kept my eyes down and my answers short.

Because how do you explain that?
How do you tell someone that school was scary—not because of bullies or homework—but because it meant leaving the only place that finally felt safe?

So, I kept it to myself.

I carried Tennessee in my chest like a locked box.
Heavy. Secret. Untouchable.

But after fifth grade, things began to shift.

I found real friends—quiet, kind kids who didn't ask too many questions, who invited me in without demanding explanations.
We passed notes in class, shared snacks at lunch, rode bikes after school.
They didn't know what I'd come from.
But they treated me like I was normal.
And part of me began to believe it.

I joined activities—school clubs, summer camp days, little things that slowly reminded me I was *allowed* to enjoy life.
That joy didn't have to come with a cost.

And I started sleeping.
Not perfectly. Not without nightmares.
But more than zero.

Some nights I still lay awake too long, listening for sounds that weren't coming.
But most nights… I rested.
My body stopped bracing.
My breath slowed down.
And I slept, not well, but better than nothing.

No one ever knew how bad it had been.
Not really.

They saw a quiet kid with a soft voice and a funny accent.
They didn't see the memories stitched into my skin.
They didn't know about the closets or the cold or the screams or the glass.

And I didn't tell them.
Not then.
Not for years.

Because saying it out loud made it real again.
And for the first time in my life, I didn't want to live in that story anymore.

I wanted to start a new one.

And in Texas—
I finally could.

## Chapter Twelve: Starting Over, Again

Eventually, my mom came to Texas too.

I don't remember how the decision was made.
Maybe it was quiet. Maybe it was desperate.
But one day, she arrived—with her bags, her tired eyes, and her own version of starting over.

We didn't talk much about Tennessee.
There was no sit-down conversation, no deep breakdown of what had happened.
Just two people—mother and daughter—trying to rebuild something from the wreckage.

We got our own apartment.
Small, basic, but *ours*.
For the first time, we had space that didn't echo with threats.
We had furniture that hadn't been smashed.
We had a fridge with food, a TV that worked, and—maybe most important of all—a *phone*.

A real landline. With a number that belonged to *us*.

It felt like a symbol.
A line out to the world.
A signal that we weren't trapped anymore.

But of course, the past has a way of finding its way back in.

Red started calling.

Sometimes the phone would ring once, twice—then silence.
Other times, I'd answer, only to hear his voice slither through the line like poison.

I'd hang up immediately.
No words.
Just the click of refusal.

He always sounded surprised.
Like he still had some piece of power.
Like maybe we were still afraid.

But I wasn't—not in the same way.

Every time I slammed that receiver down, I felt a little stronger.
It wasn't much. But it was *something.*
A now ten-year-old girl taking back what little control she could.

My mom still kept slight contact with him.
Maybe out of habit. Maybe guilt. Maybe some part of her still wasn't ready to cut the cord completely.

I didn't understand it then.
Sometimes I still don't.

But I know this:
He wasn't in our apartment.
He wasn't in our space.
And I made sure he wasn't in *my head*—not as much, not like before.

Life didn't become perfect.
But it became *possible.*

We had hard days.
Money was tight.
The shadows of the past didn't vanish just because the address changed.

But we were in Texas.
Together.
Trying.

And for the first time in my life, I wasn't just a passenger in someone else's nightmare.

I was building something of my own.

Texas felt like more than just a state—it felt like a second chance.

I started doing better in school.

Not right away.
But slowly, the panic that used to live in my chest like a second heartbeat began to loosen.
My brain, once trained only to survive, started to open itself to learning.

I could focus.
I could retain things.
I could raise my hand without fear of being mocked.

Teachers started to notice.
I wasn't the quiet, broken girl anymore.
I was the one who worked hard, the one who stayed after class to ask questions, the one who turned in neat handwriting with corners folded just right.

I wasn't the smartest kid in the room—
but I was *present.*

And that was more than I'd ever been allowed to be before.

I started enjoying school—not just the social part, but the learning itself.
History, spelling, science experiments.
I soaked up anything that reminded me I was still capable.
Still smart.
Still *here*.

And I made friends.
Real ones.
The kind who waited for me at the school gate, who passed notes during math class, who called the house just to talk about nothing at all.

We had inside jokes.
Sleepovers.
Friendship bracelets and silly arguments and whispered crushes.
All the things I never thought I'd get to experience.

At recess, I didn't sit alone.
I ran.
I chased.
I *belonged*.

And then—gymnastics.

My aunt had seen me flipping around the living room one afternoon and suggested I try a class.
At first, I was shy. I didn't think I had the right body, or enough strength, or that someone like me could ever fly.
But the second I stepped foot on that spring floor, something in me lit up.

Tumbling, leaping, stretching—my body finally got to do something *other* than hold in pain.

It got to *move* with freedom.
With joy.
With power.

Each cartwheel was a quiet rebellion.
Each backbend was proof that I wasn't broken.
Each pull on the bars, each balance on the beam—it gave me something I'd never had before:

*Trust.*
In my body.
In my strength.
In myself.

There were still hard moments.
Sometimes I'd wake from a nightmare and check the locks twice before falling back asleep.
Sometimes an unexpected noise would freeze me in place.
Sometimes I'd catch my mom staring off again, lost in whatever she still carried.

But sixth grade brought light.

It brought music.
It brought movement.
It brought *hope.*

I still hadn't told anyone the whole truth.
I still carried my past like a locked box in my chest.

But for the first time… I wasn't afraid to walk out the door.
I wasn't afraid of laughter.
I wasn't afraid of tomorrow.

And that—
was everything.

## Chapter Thirteen: What We Carried with Us

My relationship with my mom was never strong.

She loved me—deeply, no doubt about that.
But love and trust aren't always the same thing.
And while I loved her too, I could never fully agree with the decisions she made—especially when it came to the people she let into our lives… and the things she let into hers.

Leaving Tennessee had been a blessing.
It gave us space.
It gave us a new beginning.
It gave me a chance to grow, to breathe, to imagine something better.

But for her, the past followed close behind.

Her trauma didn't disappear in the Texas sun.
It just changed shape.

The drinking, which had already started back in Tennessee, continued.
At first, it was just beer. A few at night. The quiet kind of drinking.
But it never stayed that simple.

Soon it was pills.
Prescriptions—at first. Oxycodone.
Little orange bottles that came with instructions she stopped reading.
She told herself they helped. She told me they were for pain.

And maybe at first they were.
But it didn't take long before the pills became her coping mechanism.

Her escape.
Her silence.

Oxy was just the beginning.
It became the gateway to other prescriptions.
She collected bottles like armor—each one something to keep the memories numb, the guilt quiet, the grief buried.

I saw it happening.
Even as a kid, I noticed the change in her eyes.
The way her speech would slow. The way her body would slump.
The way she'd forget conversations.
The way she'd apologize and then do it again the next day.

And I hated that I understood why.

I knew what she was trying to forget.
I knew what she carried.
I knew she had never really stopped running from Red—even after we left him.

But understanding it didn't make it easier to live with.

I didn't yell.
I didn't cry.
I just got quieter. More distant.

We lived in the same apartment, but it started to feel like we were in different worlds.
Me, trying to move forward.
Her, stuck in the past.

I wanted her to choose differently.
I wanted her to choose *me*.

But she was lost in something I couldn't fix.

And still—she loved me.
Fiercely.
Flawed as she was, broken as her coping became—she loved me with everything she had left.

I felt it in the way she made sure I had clothes for school.
In the way she cheered at my gymnastics meets, even if her eyes were glassy.
In the way she'd hold my hand a little too tightly, like she was afraid I'd leave her behind.

She loved me the best way she knew how.

But I was learning that love doesn't always look like safety.
And sometimes the people who love us the most still hurt us the deepest—because they never learned how to love themselves first.

My comfort zone was always with my aunt and uncle.
They had become my foundation—the steady place I could land when everything else felt unstable.
They were the ones who came to Tennessee in that RV.
The ones who opened their doors again and again without hesitation.
The ones who gave me a second childhood when I'd barely survived the first.

When I had the choice, I chose *them.*

I chose safety.
I chose routine.
I chose a home that didn't smell like stale beer or sound like slurred apologies.

My mom and I never had that kind of home together.
There were moments, small ones, when she tried—when she got a new job, when she stayed clean for a week or two, when we laughed watching a movie or ate dinner at the table like a real family.
Those moments were rare.
And they didn't last.

There would be times I'd give her another chance.
I'd try to live with her again.
Maybe I hoped it would be different, that the shadow over her would finally lift.
I always came back hoping she'd *stay* better.
But she never could.

The pills crept back in.
The house got quiet in all the wrong ways.

Eventually, I stopped waiting for her to change.

My safe space wasn't with her—and that was a truth I had to learn early.

It wasn't because I didn't love her.
I *did.*
It wasn't because I didn't want to be close to her.
I *did.*

But I also wanted peace.
And peace didn't live with her.
It lived in my aunt and uncle's house—in warm meals, clean bedsheets, consistency, and people who kept their word.

I had to grieve that reality.
To mourn the mother I needed and didn't have, even while loving the one I got.

There was no big argument, no dramatic goodbye.
Just the slow, quiet separation of two people walking different paths.
Me, toward healing.
Her, toward whatever place she thought would make the pain stop.

I kept a soft spot for her in my heart.
But I stopped giving her the power to hurt me.

And that…
was its own kind of survival.

There was a strange kind of peace that came from finally accepting what I couldn't change.
Loving my mom from a distance gave me room to breathe.
Choosing safety—choosing *me*—was no longer something I questioned.

And in the comfort of my aunt and uncle's home,
something incredible happened:
I started becoming a version of myself that wasn't just defined by trauma.

I had space to grow.
To laugh.
To make mistakes that didn't come with danger.
To be *a kid* again.

Not the scared, silent child from Tennessee…
But the girl who was finally learning how to live.

## Chapter Fourteen: Firelight and Freedom

I was a good kid.
Quiet, really.
I stayed out of real trouble. I got decent grades. I respected adults.
But my teenage years?
They were fun.

I did the typical teenage things.
Spent a lot of time with my friends.
Laughed until my sides hurt.
Told secrets at sleepovers.
Giggled about boys we'd never talk to and worried about things that seemed like the end of the world in the moment—but weren't.

There would be entire weeks where I practically lived at my best friend's house.
Her family became my second family.
They had a fridge that was always full, a couch that always had room, and a kind of joy that felt real.

Looking back, I'd love to say we were completely innocent.
But that would be a lie.

We had *a lot* of fun.
Mischief kind of came with the territory.

Living in a small Texas town meant Friday night bonfires in the woods, late-night trips to the gas station for snacks, and blasting music from someone's old truck while we danced under the stars like nobody was watching.

We snuck out of windows.
We dared each other to talk to our crushes.

We drove dirt roads just to feel free.
Nothing malicious, nothing dangerous—just the kind of harmless rebellion that lets a teenager feel alive.

For once, I wasn't the kid with the dark past.
I was just *one of the girls.*

And in those moments, around the bonfire, with sparks flying into the night sky and laughter echoing through the trees—I felt something I had never really known before:

I felt *normal.*

Even in my teenage years—when the worst was finally behind me—I still never really thought about the future.

Not in the way other kids did.

I didn't daydream about careers.
I didn't imagine college.
I didn't see myself in a cap and gown, or walking across some big stage to pick up a diploma.

No one ever asked me what I wanted to be.
No one ever said, "You'd be great at this," or, "Have you thought about that?"
It just wasn't something that existed in my world.

I was still in survival mode... even when life got better.
The idea of building a future felt like a foreign language.
I was just beginning to feel normal in the present—how could I plan ten years down the road?

Then one day, in high school, a counselor called me in for something called a "career aptitude test."

They handed me a bubble sheet and told me to answer honestly—no wrong answers, just your natural interests.

I didn't expect much from it.
But part of me was hopeful.
Maybe it would say I should be a writer. A counselor. A teacher. Something that made sense. Something… human.

Instead—
I'll never forget reading the result.

**Bull Inseminator.**

I blinked.
I read it again.

**Bull. Inseminator.**

I stared at the paper like it had personally insulted me.

Of all the things in the world—*that's* what it thought I should be?

It felt like the universe was playing a cruel joke.
Or maybe just a small-town joke.

I remember thinking:
"Is this real? Did someone set me up? Is there really that much of a demand for… bull inseminators?"

The laugh that came out of me was so hard and unexpected, it echoed through the counselor's office.

It was the kind of laugh you don't even try to hold in.
A full-body, tears-in-your-eyes, ridiculous kind of laugh.

It didn't solve anything.
It didn't give me direction.

But it gave me *something.*

A moment to breathe.
A moment to realize that I was still figuring things out, and that was okay.

Maybe it was a sign that I wasn't *meant* to take that test seriously.
Maybe it was a reminder that my path wouldn't come from a form with fill-in-the-bubbles.

It would come from living.
From trying.
From stumbling into it, one awkward, beautiful, completely unexpected step at a time.

## Chapter Fifteen: Becoming Who She Couldn't Be

By the time I reached my late teens, my mom's addiction had only gotten worse.
The distance between us wasn't just emotional—it was survival.

She was lost, and I couldn't follow her into that darkness again.

When I was old enough, I packed up my things and left.
No fanfare.
No big send-off.
Just a quiet goodbye and the knowledge that if I didn't leave then, I might never get the chance to build something of my own.

And I *wanted* something of my own.

Eventually, I began college.
No one held my hand.
No one sent care packages.
No one filled out my FAFSA for me or paid my rent or reminded me of deadlines.

I did it all on my own.

I got a job.
Sometimes two.
I studied at night, worked during the day, and scraped by on caffeine, cheap groceries, and determination.

I decided I wanted to be a teacher.

Maybe because I had spent so many years navigating life without one—
Without someone who saw me, encouraged me, or believed in what I could become.
Maybe I wanted to *be* that for someone else.

I worked my way through college with my head down and my heart focused.
And through it all, I kept my distance from my mother.

I would call.
Sometimes she'd answer, and her voice would be slurred and distant.
Other times, she wouldn't pick up at all.
Once, I drove to see her, only to find her passed out behind a locked door.

I tried.
I begged.
I left brochures on rehab clinics.
I cried in parking lots after yet another failed intervention.

But I learned the hard truth:
You can't save someone who doesn't want to be saved.
You can scream, you can offer every lifeline in the world—
but if they don't believe they need help, nothing sticks.

That truth gutted me.

Because I wanted so badly for her to heal.
I wanted her to meet me on the other side of all this pain.

But instead, I used her life as an example of what *not* to do.

I vowed never to numb myself the way she did.
Never to put a bottle or a pill ahead of my children.
Never to create a home where fear lived in the walls.

I didn't want my children to feel the way I had felt—
Unseen. Unprotected. Unwanted.

I wanted them to know safety.
To know what a warm bed and a loving parent looked like.
To never feel like they had to parent *me.*

I kept going.

I stayed strong.

I pushed through, even on the nights I wanted to break.

And every test I passed, every paycheck I earned, every step
I took toward the life I was building—
I did it with them in mind.

The children I didn't have yet.
The family I hadn't created yet.
But the legacy I was already rewriting.

Because I wasn't just becoming a teacher.
I was becoming a mother—
*The mother I never had.*

## Chapter Sixteen: The Last Door She Couldn't Open

My mother died alone in her apartment.

Years of pill addiction chipped away at her—piece by piece—until there wasn't enough left to fight back.
What started as prescriptions for pain turned into a full dependence.
What was supposed to help her only buried her deeper.

Doctors gave her pills like candy.
Oxycodone, hydrocodone, benzos—whatever the newest "solution" was.
Each one came with promises:
"You'll feel better."
"This will help you sleep."
"This will take the edge off."

But no one ever addressed the reason she needed that edge dulled in the first place.

No one asked about the trauma.
The beatings.
The fear.
The years of silence she endured just trying to keep me safe.
No one asked if she needed therapy—just if she needed a refill.

And she always did.

Those pills were her escape.
Her comfort.
Her way of staying numb in a world that had offered her very little kindness.

She died not because she was weak—
But because no one ever showed her how to be well.

The grief was complicated.
Of course, I loved her.
Of course, I mourned her.

But I also mourned everything she *never got to become.*

She never healed.
She never got clean.
She never saw the woman I became or the peace I found.
She never got the second chance I had hoped for all those years.

And that...
It broke something in me.

Because I started to see how many others were living her story.

How many mothers, fathers, daughters, and sons were slipping through the cracks—prescribed into silence, numbed into invisibility.

Trauma. Depression. Pain.
So many turned to pills not to feel high, but to *feel nothing.*

It made me angry.

Angry that she died alone.
Angry that her death could've been prevented.
Angry that the same system that ignored her pain made a profit from it.

Big pharmaceutical companies fed off people like her—pushing pills through smiling doctors and calling it care.
And the worst part?
They knew exactly what they were doing.

She wasn't just my mom.
She was one of *millions*.
And they let her die anyway.

In the quiet that followed her passing, I made another vow—
Not just to stay away from that path, but to *fight* it.
To speak about it.
To acknowledge that addiction isn't always about weakness.
Sometimes, it's about *untreated pain*.

She didn't want to be an addict.
She wanted help.
She wanted peace.

But peace never came—at least not in the way she needed.

I carry her story now.
With sadness.
With fury.
With purpose.

Because silence didn't save her.
And maybe, just maybe, speaking the truth can help someone else.

## Chapter Seventeen: Forward, Always

Losing my mother didn't stop me.
It *fueled* me.

I didn't spiral.
I didn't fall apart.
I got focused.

I worked harder.
Not just to stay afloat, but to *build something real.*
A life that was mine.
A future that had never been promised, but that I was determined to claim.

I took on multiple jobs while going to college.
Some days I worked so much I'd come home and fall asleep in my clothes, textbooks still open on my lap.
I lived on my own.
Paid every bill.
Handled every detail.
Never asked for help—not because I didn't need it, but because I didn't know how.

There was a fire in me.
And even when I was exhausted, even when I doubted myself, that fire never went out.

I walked across that graduation stage with tears in my eyes.
Not just because I'd earned a degree.
But because I'd broken a chain.
Because every paper, every exam, every shift I worked while others partied—it all led to *this.*
Proof that I had turned pain into power.

And just two months after that, I got married.

We'd been together for years, but I'd waited.
Not because I didn't love him—but because I knew I had to accomplish *my* goals first.
I had to prove to myself that I could finish what I started.
That I could create something solid before stepping into a life partnership.

Graduation wasn't just a milestone.
It was the moment I could finally breathe.
And once that breath came, I stepped into marriage not as someone searching for stability—
But as someone who had already *built it.*

There was joy in that.
Pride.
Peace.

I wasn't trying to be anyone's savior.
I wasn't looking to be saved.

I had saved *myself.*

And in that season, I began to believe—
Not only that I had survived,
But that I had *arrived.*

## Chapter Eighteen: Building Dreams, Growing Roots

After graduation and marriage, life didn't slow down—it picked up speed.

I worked as a substitute teacher while holding down a full-time job,
pouring energy into our home,
into our future,
and into supporting my husband as he chased his dreams.

His goals mattered to me.
His success mattered to me.
And I knew what it felt like to chase something without help—
so I became the help I always wished someone had been for me.

We juggled work and business ventures,
late nights and early mornings,
deadlines and quiet moments squeezed in between.

There was no time for pause.
But there was purpose.
And there was love.

And then—
we had children.

Three beautiful souls.
Each one a piece of the future I once couldn't even imagine.

Becoming a mother was everything and nothing like I expected.
It was hard. Beautiful. Loud. Exhausting. Healing.

I didn't just see myself in them—
I saw every vow I had made to my younger self being lived out, one day at a time.

They had what I never did:
Stability.
Laughter.
Bedtime stories instead of fights behind closed doors.

They had a home filled with warmth, not fear.

And that didn't happen by accident.
It happened because I had made it *my mission* to stop the cycle.
To build the life I once prayed for while hiding in closets and clinging to hope.

There were days I felt stretched thin,
like I was pouring from an empty cup—
but I never once doubted why I was doing it.

This was the life I had fought for.

Not perfect,
but *safe.*
*Full.*
*Ours.*

## Chapter Nineteen: The Making of a Life

They say your past shapes your future.
And I used to hate that idea.

Because for a long time, I didn't want my past to shape anything.
I wanted to outrun it, erase it, rewrite it.
I didn't want to be the girl who survived violence, poverty, neglect, and fear.

But now?
I see it differently.

Because my past *did* shape my future—
but *I* decided *how*.

All the things that broke me became the reason I built something better.
All the nights I couldn't sleep became the fuel behind my ambition. All the things I didn't have… became the exact things I vowed to give.

To my children.
To myself.
To the people I reach through my work.

I'm not in a classroom today.
Not in the way I once imagined.

But life, for me, is still full of lessons.
And I am still teaching—just in different ways.

I am an entrepreneur now.
My husband and I have built multiple businesses from the ground up.
We've learned how to dream together, struggle together, *win* together.

It wasn't handed to us.
It was earned.
Hour by hour, sacrifice by sacrifice.

And every ounce of success we've built didn't come *in spite* of my past—
it came *because* I knew what it meant to have nothing.

I knew what it meant to go without.
To want more.
To crave safety and freedom so deeply that it became a mission.

And now I get to live that mission.

We've built something that matters.
Something stable.
Something rooted in love and grit and *never giving up.*

## Chapter Twenty: The Sound of Freedom

I sit outside on a warm afternoon, the golden sun resting gently on the shoulders of my children as they race down the sidewalk on their scooters—laughing, yelling to their friends, their voices echoing pure, innocent joy.

Their cheeks are flushed.
Their hair is wild from the wind.
Their hands are sticky from popsicles, and not a care in the world rests on their small, bright shoulders.

And I watch them—not just with love, but with *awe*.

Because this is everything I fought for.

They are living a life I only dreamed of at their age.
They are free.
Free from fear.
Free from trauma.

They don't hide in closets.
They don't flinch when doors slam.
They don't worry if there will be food on the table or safety when the sun goes down.

They are whole.

And that is because *I* decided the cycle would end with me.

They ride scooters.
I once ran barefoot through the night to escape violence.

They play tag.
I once held my breath under bedsheets, praying for the screaming to stop.

They build forts.
I once built emotional walls so tall no one could reach me.

But here we are.

Generational trauma is real.
But so is **generational healing**.

And I chose healing.

When I look at my children, I don't just see them.
I see *me*.
The me that didn't give up.
The me that clawed her way out of fear.
The me that worked multiple jobs, put herself through school, said "no" when it would've been easier to say "fine," and made the painful choice to keep distance from people I loved because I knew I needed to protect myself.

I see the little girl I used to be, standing tall in the mother I've become.

This life didn't come wrapped in ease or handed down through comfort.
It came from years of scraping together strength from broken places.
It came from knowing what I *didn't* want, and using that as a blueprint for what I would *never* allow again.

And to **anyone** reading this who is carrying a silent battle:
You are not alone.

You are not broken.
You are *becoming.*

Maybe your story has been heavy.
Maybe your past still wakes you up at night.
Maybe the world has told you that survival is the best you can hope for.

But I'm here to tell you:
You can *thrive.*
You can build a life so different, so beautiful, that it makes your pain feel like it happened to someone else.

Not because it wasn't real.
But because *you were stronger.*

You can be the first in your family to heal.
You can be the safe parent.
You can live in a home that feels like peace—not because it's perfect, but because *you made it safe.*

Keep going.
Keep choosing yourself.
Keep choosing peace.
Keep choosing love—even when you've only ever known pain.

Because one day, you'll look out your window and see your children playing—
laughing like their little hearts have never known hurt—
and you'll realize:
**This is it.**

This is the moment everything changed.

And it started with *you.*

**To the Reader: A Lesson in Survival**

If you're reading this and you're still in the storm—
I want you to know something:

**You can survive it.**
And not just survive it—*grow from it.*
Use it.
Shape it into something new.

Your story doesn't have to end in the same place it began.
Your trauma does not have to be your identity.

You *can* be the one who breaks the cycle.
You *can* build the life you were never given.
You *can* give your children what you didn't receive.

It will be hard.
It will take every ounce of strength you have.
You will cry. You will doubt. You will fall.

But if you keep going—
One decision at a time,
One breath at a time,
One brave step at a time—
You will look up one day and realize you did it.

Not because it was easy.
But because *you refused to quit.*

That's what I hope this story shows.

That a little girl once hid in a closet with her dog, afraid of what the night might bring—

and now she runs businesses, raises children, and builds *legacy*.

That trauma doesn't have to be the end.
It can be the beginning.

Keep going.
Keep believing.
Keep building.
Even if no one else believes in you—*believe in yourself*.

Because you are capable.
You are worthy.
And you are *living proof*
that pain is not the end of the story.

## Epilogue – The Long Road Back

The air in Tennessee felt heavier than I remembered. It wasn't just the humidity—though that clung to my skin the moment I stepped out of the rental car—it was the weight of everything this place carried for me. Every memory, every shadow, every sound from the past seemed to hum beneath the surface. I was here for a reason, one that felt both sacred and impossible: to spread my mother's and my aunt's ashes.

I had avoided coming back for so many years. I told myself there was no reason, that my life was in Texas now, that nothing good could come from retracing steps that had been soaked in fear. But deep down, I think I knew I would eventually have to stand here again—to see what remained and what had been erased, to let my past know I survived it.

The closer we drove toward my childhood home, the more I felt that familiar, queasy mix of dread and curiosity. I wondered how much had changed. I wondered if I'd still recognize anything at all.

When we turned onto the street, my chest tightened.

The house was gone.
In its place stood a new one—modern, clean-lined, with fresh siding and shutters that looked like they'd never known rot or chipped paint. It was… different. Safer, maybe. But my mind's eye still painted the picture of what used to be there—the sagging roof, the peeling trim, the broken blinds swaying in the windows. The old place had been knocked down, but in its absence, it was as if a ghost version still lingered, superimposed over the new construction.

And then I saw it.

The fence.
The exact same fence that had stood there decades ago, its metal weathered and leaning in places but still holding strong.

And the clothesline—thin, sagging slightly under the years—was still there too. The same one my mom used to hang our clothes on. I could almost see her in my mind's eye, standing there with clothespins in her mouth, her one good arm stretching shirts across the line while the half-length arm, the result of that childhood accident, held the fabric steady. She'd still somehow do it all—guarding me with a fierceness that didn't need two full arms to make it powerful.

The sight of that clothesline did something to me. It was proof that some things endure—not because they're unbreakable, but because they're rooted deep enough to withstand storms. In a strange way, I realized that clothesline was me. Weathered, maybe bent, but still standing.

I walked toward the back, heart pounding in my ears. And there it was—the gulley.
The place where I'd run to escape more nights than I could count. The place where my feet had pounded across the footbridge in pure, unfiltered terror. Except… the bridge wasn't there anymore.

What was left of it lay crumbled in the gulley below, giant chunks of cement scattered like bones. The cement that had once rattled beneath my small, fleeing feet were gone entirely. Time had done to that bridge what years of running could not—it had broken it down to nothing. I stood there staring at the pieces, thinking about all the nights I'd flown across it, feeling the boards give slightly under my steps, praying I wouldn't fall before I made it to safety.

Back then, that bridge had been my lifeline.
Now, seeing it in ruins, I felt… complicated.
Sadness, yes. But also an understanding. That bridge had served its purpose, over and over, until it couldn't anymore. And maybe that was okay. Maybe its fall into the gulley was a kind of rest, the same way I'd eventually been allowed to stop running.

I stood there for a long time, the wind rustling the weeds that had grown wild around the broken cement.

And as I looked out over the gulley, I thought about the ashes I carried in my bag. I traveled down the street where my mother and aunts' childhood home was, less than a mile from my childhood home

Spreading my mother's and my aunt's ashes here felt right. They had the fondest moments at their childhood home unlike me. They'd known laughter, inside jokes, and small joys that made them best friends. Leaving a part of them here felt like acknowledging it all—the good and the bad, the love and the loss.

I opened the urn, the wind catching the ashes and carrying them over the grass, across the fence line, into the air. My throat tightened. I thought of my mother—her stubbornness, her flaws, her impossible love for me even when her addiction built walls between us. I thought of the way she'd guarded me with all she had, half an arm or not, and how much of my strength came from watching her survive what she did.

Then I thought about my aunt, how she was the anchor in the storm, the person who had opened her home to me, fed me, made me feel safe. I thought of the summer of 1992, when I cried so hard in her shower that she helped make a plan to save me. I owed her so much more than I could ever say.

When both urns were empty, I closed my eyes. The air was still for a moment, like even Tennessee was holding its breath.

And then, as if the past wasn't done with me yet, I remembered what I had learned not long before making this trip: **Red was dead.**
November. Cancer.

When I first heard, I felt something I couldn't name at first. Then it came in waves. Relief. A flood of it—because I knew he could never hurt anyone again. Not a child. Not a woman. Not me.

But almost as quickly, another feeling rose up—anger. Anger that he had lived as long as he did, longer than my mother. Anger that he had stolen so much from me and still had years I wished could have gone to someone better. And buried under all that was this small, stubborn shard of disappointment. I had always imagined that one day, as an adult, I would get to look him in the eye and tell him what he'd done to me. I thought I'd have that confrontation, that moment of taking back some power. His death stole that, too.

I know some people would tell me to let that go, to focus on the fact that he was gone, that I was free. And in many ways, I have. But healing is never clean. Relief and rage can live in the same breath. Closure doesn't always feel like victory—it often feels like an unfinished sentence you'll never get to complete.

Standing there at the gulley, I thought about all the pieces of my life that were still here in Tennessee—the fence, the clothesline, the crumbled bridge. And I realized that those pieces weren't just relics of trauma. They were proof of survival. They were markers of the path I had run, the path that led me away, the path that—against all odds—brought me back standing on my own two feet.

I left Tennessee that day with something I hadn't expected: a sense of ownership over my own story.
For years, I had avoided this place, thinking it belonged to my pain. But now I understood—it belonged to me. The memories here were mine, but so was the survival. So was the perseverance. So was the ending.

And maybe, just maybe, coming back wasn't about finding closure at all.
Maybe it was about planting my feet on the ground where I once ran barefoot in fear, and knowing that I don't have to run anymore.

## Thank You for Reading

Thank you for spending your time with *Silent Battle.*
If this book moved you, encouraged you, or made you feel seen, I would be truly grateful if you left a review.

Reviews help this story reach the readers who need it most and support independent authors in continuing to create meaningful work.

Thank you for reading — and for your support.

**— Olivia Paisley Troy**

www.ingramcontent.com/pod-product-compliance
Lightning Source LLC
LaVergne TN
LVHW020048110826
845155LV00029B/678

* 9 7 9 8 9 9 3 6 4 7 5 0 0 *